KT-379-558

Manhood

is a serious business

This book is for all the men I have known,
past, present and future.

This edition published in the United Kingdom in 2014 by
Portico
1 Gower Street
London
WC1E 6HD

An imprint of Pavilion Books Company Ltd

ISBN 978 1 90939 639 5

A CIP catalogue record for this book is available from the British Library.

10 9 8 7 6 5 4 3

Design: Suzanne Perkins/grafica
Colour reproduction by Dot Gradations Ltd, UK
Printed and bound by GPS Printing Ltd, Slovenia
This book can be ordered direct from the publisher at www.pavilionbooks.com

THE WIT AND

Cath Tate

WISDOM OF

Manhood

is a serious business

PORTICO

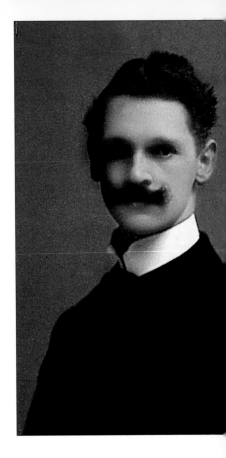

Manhood is a
very serious business.

God made man
in his own image.

Fashionable elegance and charm define the modern man.

A man won't get far without his mates.

Men discuss things women
don't even think about.

Men are like computers. You never know what's going on inside.

It's good to go out and have
a laugh with the lads.

Men rule the world,

once women have sorted
everything out.

But can they boil an egg?

"I was meant to lead the revolution, not teach."

"I'm a man of the people.
I clean my own moat."

Men don't grow old: they just become more important.

Men don't go for a pint.
They're "Networking".

The most important
question to ask a man is
how he combines a family
and a career.

Fatherhood?
There's nothing to it!

"When I grow up I'm going to have my own band."

"I can't do the washing up, my voice has broken."

"I'm up and dressed!
What more do you want?"

If only girls came with
drop-down menus and
online help…

You finally become a man when you've mastered the washing machine.

The best things in
life are free.

The second best cost loads of money.

At last he was able
to get his own place.

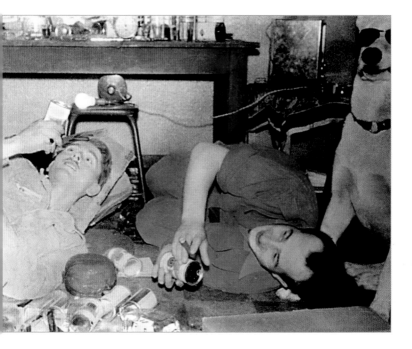

We have everything a woman could want except money, talent and looks.

There are few things
more fetching than a
man in shorts.

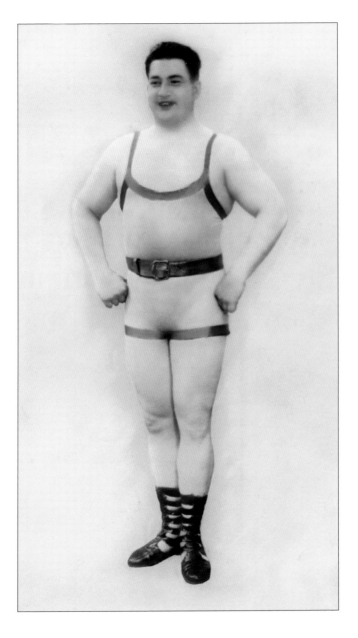

M with GSOH
seeks slim, attract.
lady, 20 – 35, for romantic
evenings, log fires and
maybe more.

Man with GSOH seeks stable relationship.

Never use your
passport photo for your
online dating page.

"Thailand to buy myself
a wife."

When a man
opens a car door
for a woman,
either the woman
or the car is new.

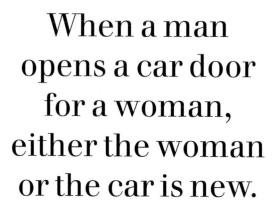

Most men would be
happily married if only
their wives were cars.

Never argue with a woman
she's always right

Never argue with a man:
he's always wrong.

If you pay for the
meal, you don't have
to laugh at his jokes.

A man in the kitchen: perfection on the stove, bombsite in the sink.

Nothing gives
more pleasure than a
new sound system.

"Nobody knows I'm Elvis."

There's nothing more enjoyable than trying to get something useless to work.

Eventually he stopped playing computer games and got a proper job.

Instruction manuals are for wimps.

If only he would ask
directions…

There's a fine line between fishing and standing on the shore looking like an idiot.

You can tell a happy cyclist by the flies on his teeth.

If everything is under control you're obviously not going fast enough.

"Some people think football is a matter of life and death…
it's much more serious than that."

BILL SHANKLY

"I spent a lot of money on booze, birds and fast cars. The rest I just squandered."

GEORGE BEST

All men over 40
are scoundrels.

It is better to be silent and thought a fool, than to speak out and remove all doubt.

"I used to be an atheist until I realised I *was* God."

Talk to a man about himself and he will listen for hours.

"I told you I was ill!"

You have to
take men as they are…

…and then go to work
on them.

"Men!
I've been looking for a solution for years."

Behind every woman
stands a man wondering
what he said wrong.

Women like the simple things in life, like men.

Men are like wine:
they reach perfection
with age.

Cath Tate has lived and worked in London for more years than she cares to mention. She currently runs a greeting card company, Cath Tate Cards, with her daughter Rosie: the bulk of the photos and captions in this book started life as greetings cards.

The photos have been collected over the years by Cath and her friends in junk shops and vintage fairs. They are all genuine and show people in all their glory, on the beach, on a day out, posing stiffly for the photographer, drinking with friends, smiling or scowling at the camera.

The photographs were all taken sometime between 1880 and 1960. Times change but people, their friendships, their little joys and stupid mistakes, remain the same. Some things have changed though, and Cath Tate has used modern technical wizardry to tease some colour into the cheeks of those whose cheeks lost their colour some time ago.

The quotes that go with the photos come from random corners of life and usually reflect some current concern that is bugging her.

If you want to see all the current greetings cards and other ephemera available from Cath Tate Cards see www.cathtatecards.com

Cath Tate

Many thanks to all those helped me put this book together, including Discordia, who have fed me with wonderful photos and ideas over the years, and Suzanne Perkins, who has made sure everything looks OK, and also has a good line in jokes.

Picture credits

Photos from the collection of Cath Tate apart from the following:
Discordia/Simon: Pages 2–3, 4–5, 12–13, 16–17, 18–19, 24–25, 30–31, 40–41, 42–43, 44–45, 46–47, 60–61, 62–63, 66–67, 68–69, 70–71, 72–73, 76–77, 100–101, 108–109
Discordia/Siegmann: Pages 48–49, 58–59, 86–87
Keith Allen: Pages 36–37